MILLENNIUM CITY

Once in a thousand years...a Chicago

A proud city of Irish- African- Polish- Italian- Chinese-
Greek- Mexican- German- Thai-Jewish- Japanese-
English. Fairly swarming with hyphenated Americans,
yet not at all a melting pot. Rather a collection of
neighborhoods, intact, comfortable, and welcoming.
Chicago enters the twenty-first century proud of
its heritage, proud of the hardships overcome and
confident of its future as a World City of the first rank.
But it was a long, often bumpy road.

More than three hundred years ago...

explorers moving from east to west across North
America discovered the distance between the
Checagou River and the Des Plaines River to be only
a few thousand yards, easily portaged by travelers
in canoes. The Checagou connected with the east
coast via the Great Lakes; the Des Plaines with the
Mississippi and the western rivers. The place was
important, and so the Checagou Portage, named
after a wild onion, became the town of Chicago.

In 1674, the explorers Marquette and Joliet passed
this way. LaSalle came in 1682 and claimed all the
land touched by the Mississippi and its tributaries for
France. He named it "Louisiana," after King Louis XIV.

The first non-native settler, in 1779, was Jean-Baptiste
Point DuSable, a black man from the Caribbean
island of Hispaniola. He was a successful trader who
built a cabin roughly where the original **Prudential
Building** stands, took a Potowatomi bride, raised
three children, and saw the birth of a grandchild
before departing for Missouri in 1804.

Fort Dearborn was built in 1803 at the present south
end of the Michigan Avenue Bridge, where a *bas
relief* on the bridge tower recalls the Ft. Dearborn
Massacre in 1812. The native Americans of the
Midwest, led by the charismatic Shawnee chief,
Tecumseh, had united with the English to make war
against the fledgling United States.

Just six years later in 1818, Illinois was admitted to
the Union as the twenty-first state. Chicago was in a
period of slow but steady growth as enthusiastic
settlers moved westward seeking cheap and
fertile land. Speculators followed, making Chicago
a typical "boom and bust" town. The linkage by
water between the manufacturers of the East and
the markets of the West was finally achieved in 1848,
when the Illinois-Michigan Canal was completed. In
1860, **Abe Lincoln** was nominated for the presidency
in Chicago, and by the end of the Civil War the city
was almost as big as St. Louis. The Union Stockyards

*The setting sun wraps the city centre in a glittering
golden shadow.*

Chicago Timeline

1673	Discovery	1885	First Skyscraper	1942	December 2 — First Controlled Atomic Reaction
1779	Jean-Baptiste Point du Sable	1886	The Haymarket Riot	1943	Chicago's First Subway Opened
1803-12	The First Fort Dearborn	1888	Jane Addams — Hull House	1955	Richard J. Daley Elected Mayor
1818	Illinois Admitted to Statehood	1893	World's Columbian Exposition	1956	Congress Expressway Opened
1833	Incorporated as a Town	1900	Flow of Chicago River Reversed		— Renamed Dwight D. Eisenhower
1837	Incorporated as a City		Includes brief history of the Sanitary		Expressway January 10, 1964
1840	Free Schools Established		District of Greater Chicago and the	1958	International Trade Fair Celebrates
1848	Illinois & Michigan Canal Completed		present Tunnel and Reservoir Project		Opening of St. Lawrence Seaway
1848	First City Hall in State Street		(TARP).		— Queen Elizabeth's Visit
1855	Police Department Created	1903	Iroquois Theater Fire	1966	Civic Center Dedicated — December
1860	First National Political Convention	1907	First American Nobel Prize		27, 1976 Renamed the Richard J.
	— Abraham Lincoln Nominated		Winner in Science From University		Daley Center
1861-65	The Civil War		of Chicago	1967	August 15 — Picasso Statue Unveiled
1865	Chicago Union Stock Yard Completed	1908	Chicago Plan Published — First		In Civic Center Plaza
1867	The First Tunnel Under the Lake		Comprehensive Outline Offered To An	1973	Sears Tower Completed
1868	Chicago Water Tower		American City	1976	Mayor Richard J. Daley Dies at 74
1871	The Great Fire	1915	Eastland Disaster	1983	Harold Washington is Elected Mayor
1872	Montgomery Ward — First Mail-Order House	1927	Municipal Airport of Chicago (Midway) Opened	1989	Richard M. Daley Elected Mayor
1873	Chicago Public Library (CPL) Opened	1933-34	A Century of Progress	2004	Millennium Park Opened

Left: Chicago in 1832: Wolf Point. Lithograph from a drawing by George Davis. Creator: Rufus Blanchard.

Below: Rush Street Bridge on the turn of the Chicago River; ca. 1869. Photo by J. Carbutt.

opened in 1865, giving Chicago its character as "hog butcher to the world," and providing jobs for generations of immigrant workers.

The Great Chicago Fire

When fire swept through in 1871, the city had a population of 300,000. The blaze cleansed Chicago of its ramshakle slums, riverfront saloons, and wooden sidewalks. It also destroyed the graceful old homes and worthy commercial buildings, but the catastrophe created an opportunity unique among great cities to begin anew.

The late years of the century saw unparalleled growth for the City of Chicago despite a series of labor troubles, culminating in the notorious Haymarket Riot of 1885. That same year saw completion of the prototype of the modern skyscraper, the **Home Insurance Building**, designed by William LeBaron Jenny, towering all of *ten stories* above the intersection of Adams and LaSalle Streets. **The Rookery** opened the next year, eleven floors with six hundred offices, right across the street. It still stands, a monument to

CHICAGO

Text by
David Stockwell

Photos by
Karina Wang

Project and editorial conception: Casa Editrice Bonechi
Publication Manager: Monica Bonechi
Picture research: Monica Bonechi. *Cover:* Manuela Ranfagni
Graphic design and make-up: Laura Settesoldi *and* Manuela Ranfagni. *Editing:* Simonetta Giorgi
Map page 44 by Stefano Benini
City map by Lawrence Okrent

Text: David Stockwell

© Copyright by Casa Editrice Bonechi Florence - Italy
E-mail:bonechi@bonechi.it

Printed in Italy by Centro Stampa Editoriale Bonechi.

The photographs from the Archives of Casa Editrice Bonechi *are by* Karina Wang.

Pages 4 and 5: © Chicago Historical Society.
Aerial Photo on page 45: Lawrence Okrent.
Pages 56 and 57 top: © The Art Institute of Chicago.
Pages 60 bottom and 61 top and bottom: courtesy of the Field Museum of Natural History, *Chicago.*
Pages 63 and 64 top: courtesy of © The Adler Planetarium.
Pages 66 and 67: © Museum of Science and Industry, *Chicago.*

ISBN 978-88-476-1817-6
www.bonechi.com

* * *

designers Daniel Burnham and
John Root.

The Columbian Exposition

Enjoying a population of more
than a million in 1890, Chicago
was chosen to host the World's
Fair in 1892, celebrating the
four hundredth anniversary of
the discovery of America by
Christopher Columbus. The
Exposition put the city on the
international map with its **White
City** of modern architecture. One
of the noble buildings survives
today as the **Museum of Science
and Industry**.

The "Roaring Twenties"

In 1919, Alphonse Capone left
New York City and came to
Chicago. During the Prohibition
years, crime flourished, and
Chicago gained a reputation for
lawlessness, memories of which
still linger.

The "Bullish Nineties"

Happily, Michael Jordan has in
recent years bumped Alphonse to
second place as Chicago's best
known citizen. His graceful statue
can be admired just east of the
United Center.

The Atomic Age

A distinguished American of
Italian descent, Enrico Fermi,
succeeded in splitting the atom in
a squash court on the campus of
the University of Chicago in 1942.
An interesting sculpture by Henry
Moore marks the site on the Hyde
Park campus.
In 1955, Richard J. Daley was first
elected mayor. He served longer
than any other mayor, until his
death in 1976. In the mid-'60s, the
Civil Rights Movement centered
for a time on Chicago with the
visit of Martin Luther King in
1966 and the riots during the
Democratic Party Convention of
1968.
More recently, we have seen
the election of Jane Byrne, the
city's first woman chief executive
and Harold Washington, the
first African-American mayor.
Richard M. Daley, son of Richard J.,
became mayor in 1989.

*State Street looking north from Madison
Street; ca. 1905. Photo by Barnes-Crosby.*

*Following two pages:
A night view of Chicago.*

Chicago Today

Today's Chicago offers
sophisticated dining with almost
every international cuisine ably
represented. One can easily
spend $500 on dinner for two
(including a *nice* wine) at a four
star French restaurant. One can
also relish the world's very best
pizza and a glass of good beers
for about ten bucks. Four major
universities assure the continuing
presence of intelligent speakers
and other cultural activities. The
world class Chicago Symphony
Orchestra and Lyric Opera
crown the fall-winter season, and
a variety of summer festivals
explore almost all types of music
from classical to blues. Shopping,
theater, spectator sports, and a
great variety of tours by bus, boat,
and foot are here for the visitor.

WALT DISNEY

Walter Elias Disney was born in
Chicago on December 5, 1901.
His father, Elias Disney, was Irish-Ca-
nadian. His mother, Flora Disney, was
German-American. Walt was one of five
children, four boys and a girl. Walt early
became interested in drawing, selling
his first sketches to neighbors when he
was only seven years old. After the war,
Walt began his career as an adverti-
sing cartoonist. In 1920, he created and
marketed his first original animated
cartoons, and later perfected a new
method for combining live action and
animation.
Mickey Mouse was created in 1928,
and his talents were first used in a silent
cartoon entitled "Plane Crazy." However, Mickey made his screen debut
in "Steamboat Willie," the world's first
sound cartoon, which premiered at the
Colony Theatre in New York on Novem-
ber 18, 1928.
Disney died on December 15, 1966.

Facing page: The Chicago River flowing south. The Loop is on the left bank; River West is on the right bank.

The Loop viewed from the southeast with Grant Park in the foreground.

THE LOOP

The Loop was named for a rectangular section of elevated tracks which transport modern air conditioned Chicago Transit Authority electric trains around the central city and send them to neighborhoods and suburbs to the north, west, and south. "State Street, that great street" is the main street of the Loop.
Formerly the retail shopping hub of the midwest, State Street still boasts the flagship stores of **Marshall Field** and **Carson Pirie Scott**, but the main shopping frenzy has moved to North Michigan Avenue.

The eastern edge of the Loop is Michigan Avenue where you'll find the splendid new **Symphony Center**, home of the elite Chicago Symphony Orchestra...and a little farther north is the exciting **Chicago Cultural Center**, at Washington Street, a must stop for visitors. This neoclassical palazzo offers free programs of dance, concerts, films, lectures, and exhibits as well as high quality memorabilia available at the *Visitor Information Center*.

Some Architectural Gems

Looming over the south end of State Street is the **Harold Washington Library Center**, the world's second largest public library. Only London's British Library is larger. A visitor then might stroll west on Jackson Boulevard to **The Monadnock Building** (53 West), once the world's tallest at sixteen stories, and further west to the **Board of Trade Building** (141 West) where a tour is availalble of the trading floor. North on LaSalle is **The Rookery**; check out the lobby, redesigned by Frank Lloyd Wright in 1905.

Then double back to Dearborn Street and turn left. Note the **Marquette Building** at 140 North with its *bas relief* sculptured facade over the entrance. Across the street at Monroe stands the **Inland Steel Building**. It is hard to believe this very modern structure was built in 1954. Across Dearborn at Madison soars the graceful curving profile of the **Bank One Building**. Turn left one block north on Washington and the **Richard J. Daley Center** (City Hall) is revealed behind the famous Picasso statue. Walk a block more

to Randolph Street and turn left to view the interesting **James R. Thompson Center** (State of Illinois Building) designed by Helmut Jahn.

Other buildings of historical interest, and there are many, include **Carson Pirie Scott & Co.** at State and Madison designed by Louis Sullivan. The corner clock, a block north at Washington, the signature piece for **Marshall Field & Co.**, has been a rendezvous for generations of Chicagoans. ''I'll meet you under the clock.''

SEARS TOWER

While it is true that somebody built a building in Malaysia that has a superstructure reaching slightly higher, competitive Chicagoans take comfort in the fact that Sears' *110 habitable floors* are taller than their habitable floors. So, is it the world's tallest? Chicagoans still think so.

It is surely Chicago's number one tourist attraction. The spectactular observation deck has its own entrance on Jackson Boulevard. Designed by architect Bruce Graham and engineer Fazlur Kahn of Skidmore, Owings, and Merrill, the same team which created the John Hancock Building, to be Sears national headquarters in 1974.

Above: 333 Wacker Drive and Leo Burnett Building.

Preceding pages: Chicago's skyline seen from Lake Michigan.

Facing page: above right: Town Homes in the Dearborn Park area. Left: Tribune Tower and the Wrigley Building. Below: once the first skyscraper built after WWII, the Prudential Building is neighbor to the giant AON Building and the new 2 Prudential Plaza to the east and the Smurfit Stone Building to the west.

ARCHITECTURE AND BUILDINGS

"Make no little plans...
they have no magic to stir men's blood. Make big plans, aim high and hope... Remember that our sons and grandsons are going to do things that would stagger us."

Chicago's motto was expressed by an architect, Daniel Burnham, whose buildings stand today among the city's most cherished. He led the group of architects who designed **White City**, which became the site of the Columbian Exposition in 1890. Burnham was also the author of a "Plan of Chicago," issued in 1909, which, among many other things, assured the city of a lakefront unobstructed by buildings and other commercial development. Instead, beautiful parks: Lincoln, Grant, and Jackson line Lake Michigan from north to south.

Other architects whose work is highly visible in Chicago include Frank Lloyd Wright, Mies van der Rohe, and Helmut Jahn.

Wright was a designer, primarily of small buildings and family homes. The Chicago suburb of Oak Park, where Wright lived and worked, is the site of many Wright homes; the world famous **Robie House** stands proudly on the campus of the University of Chicago. His extraordinary genius is also in evidence in the lobby of **The Rookery** building in Chicago.

Mies came to the city in the nineteen thirties to head the Architecture Department at the Illinois Institute of Chicago. He is best known for the tall buildings he created himself and many others built in the 1960s and 1970s which were inspired by his carefully ordered style. These include the graceful **Lake Point Tower**, the **John Hancock Center**, and the **Sears Tower**. Prominent buildings designed by Mies himself include the apartment buildings at **900 and 910 Lake Shore Drive**, the **Kluczynski** and **Dirksen Federal Buildings** and the **IBM Building**. Mies is the author of the cryptic minimalist assertion, "Less is more."

Helmut Jahn is an architect of the 1980s and '90s. Glass is his medium, evidenced in the spectacular **One South Wacker Building**, the **Northwestern Atrium Center**, and the **James R. Thompson Center**. Jahn's most famous Chicago design, however, may very well prove to be the **United Airlines Terminal One Complex** at O'Hare Airport.

MILLENNIUM PARK

LOOKING FORWARD TO A GREATER CENTURY FOR CHICAGO

Since the Great Chicago Fire destroyed much of the city in 1871, a spirit of "I will," has prevailed here. Building and rebuilding Chicago never stops. From the graceful Doric-style columns to the four concealed photocell stations that provide solar power to produce electricity, **Millennium Park** brings the future into the present while honoring the past. Generous private and business donors are named throughout the park. Civic leaders and business donors: Pritzker, Crown, Harris, Wrigley, and Lurie, SBC, BP, Excelon, and Chicago Tribune.

The BP Bridge...a pedestrian walkway of stainless steel panels that's fun to travel. Children love its banks and curves. It shields concert audiences from traffic noise. Designed by Frank Gehry as a companion piece to the music pavilion.

PRITZKER MUSIC PAVILION

Architect Frank Gehry's unique design features a billowing cluster of stainless steel "petals" jutting 120 feet into the sky. It frames the concert stage, connects to a trellis of tubing which supports an array of speakers, and provides the most natural outdoor sound. 4,000 seats and lawn space for 7,000 lie beneath this acoustical canopy. Concerts are frequent and free.

Michigan Avenue

Monroe Street

The Crown Fountain

Grant Park North Garage

McCormick Tribune Plaza and Ice Rink

Park Grill Restaurant

Wringley Square

South Terrace

Cloud Gate (Sculpture)

North Terrace

Chase Promenade South

Chase Promenade Central

Chase Promenade North

AT&T Plaza

Exelon Pavilion Welcome Center

Exelon Pavilion
Millennium Garage

The Lurie Garden

Great Lawn

Roof Terrace

Jay Pritzker Pavilion

Harris Theater for Music and Dance

Exelon Pavilion
Millennium Garage

Exelon Pavilion
Millennium Garage

BP Bridge

Bike Station

Columbus Drive

Randolph Street

The new Museum of Contemporary Art. Bottom left: Chicago Historical Society. Bottom right: Chicago Cultural Center.

MUSEUM OF CONTEMPORARY ART

Chicago's **Museum of Contemporary Art** is the youngest member of the local fine arts family, founded in 1967 and occupying its present building since 1996. The **MCA** is commited to exhibiting art of the present. It is a laboratory—experimenting, informing and illuminating the nature of contemporary art. Located just east of the famous **Water Tower**, the museum presents a wide range of visual and performance art by established artists: Duchamp, Ernst, Miró, Dubuffet, and Warhol as well as cutting edge work by Paschke, Golub, and Nutt. A terraced outdoor sculpture garden faces Lake Michigan to the east.

Above: Lorado Taft's Fountain of Time, 1922.

Right: Henry Moore's "Nuclear Energy", 1967.

FOUNTAIN OF TIME

This massive (110 foot) wave of humanity stands at the western end of the Midway Plaisance. "Time," the lonely sentinel, stands across a pool of water from one hundred individual figures—soldiers, refugees, lovers, youngsters, oldsters, and includes the sculptor himself, Lorado Taft, and his assistants. **Fountain of Time** was cast in a mold made of 4,500 pieces, formed of what was then, in 1922, a new material: steel-reinforced hollow-cast concrete, which was supposed to stand the test of time. Sadly, it has not, and the surface of the sculpture is in appalling condition due to the stresses of weather and air pollution. So far, the money that would be necessary to restore it has not been found.

"NUCLEAR ENERGY"

Set on the very spot where Enrico Fermi and his team devised the first nuclear reactor is this massive twelve-foot bronze, Moore's imposing work suggests at once a protective helmet, a human skull, and a mushroom-shaped cloud.

UNIVERSITY OF CHICAGO CAMPUS

One of America's finest universities is located in Hyde Park, a south side neighborhood with sharply defined borders: Cottage Grove Avenue on the west to the Lake—and Hyde Park Blvd. (51st Street) on the north to the Midway Plaisance. Founded with generous funding from John D. Rockefeller in the 1890s, the **University of Chicago** has produced more Nobel Prize winners than any other university. Many of the prizes came in Economics, a field in which the "Chicago School" is well known.

The architect, Henry Ives Cobb, planned the campus as six broken quadrangles of strictly Gothic buildings, constructed on land donated by Marshall Field. Cobb was much influenced by the University trustees who felt Gothic had ecclesiastical and educational traditions which made it a more appropriate style for a university than Romanesque, which was high fashion in the 1890s. What followed was a forty-year Gothic building spree and a campus which is *not* made for automobiles: one has to walk the quadrangles. They're very beautiful, very traditional, with a fine selection of outdoor sculptures. A few post WW II buildings nearby break the Gothic mode.

Three views of the University of Chicago Campus.

OAK PARK

For those interested in the work of Frank Lloyd Wright, the Village of **Oak Park**, west of Chicago, is a treasure trove beyond imagining. The village was settled in the years following the Chicago Fire of 1871. It was an island of purity, free from alcohol, immigrants, and other "bringers of moral decay." It was established as an independent village in 1902. It was home not only to Wright but to authors Ernest Hemingway and Edgar Rice Burroughs, creator of the "Tarzan" books. Today, Oak Park is economically stable, integrated and progressive; home to well-educated leaders of the Chicagoland community.

For the Frank Lloyd Wright *aficionados*, everything is well organized; many guided tours are available. The best place to begin is the **Visitors Center** at 158 N. Forest Avenue. It is open every day from 10 to 5 (4 p.m. in winter) and provides orientation, maps, guidebooks, and gift items. Of more than 270 houses created by Wright, 26 are located in Oak Park and adjacent River Forest. In addition, the **Unity Temple**, one of his most famous buildings, is located just a block east of the Visitors Center.

Frank Lloyd Wright's Home and Studio

Wright's **Home and Studio** was begun in 1889. Here, Wright lived and worked for twenty years, raised six children with his first wife, Catherine Tobin, and established what is known as the "Prairie School" of architecture.

The house was completed in 1895 with the addition of a dining room and a kitchen/playroom. The studio addition went up in 1898. It showcases Wright's love of geometric shapes. After Wright left Oak Park, he remodeled the studio as living quarters for the family.
Later the buildings were remodeled into six apartments and rented out. In 1974, the complex was acquired by the National Trust for Historic

Below: Frank Lloyd Wright's home and studio in Oak Park.

Above: Wright's Heurtley House in Oak Park.

Left: Wrights Unity Temple in Oak Park.

Preservation and restored by the Frank Lloyd Wright Home and Studio Foundation to its 1905-09 appearance.

Frank Lloyd Wright arrived in Chicago in 1886 from rural Wisconsin when he was nineteen, the child of a "progressive" mother and a musician father. He apprenticed first with J.L. Silsbee, primarily a house designer, and then was hired as a draftsman by the firm of Adler and Sullivan. Louis Sullivan, probably the most famous architect of his time,`` became Wright's mentor and collaborator on several landmark designs. Wright worked on the design for Chicago's **Auditorium building**, designed by Sullivan. He opened his own office in 1893 and continued to work and experiment for 66 years until his death in 1959.

Heurtley House

The **Heurtley House** at 318 N. Forest Avenue is one of Wright's most magnificent homes. The living rooms are raised to enable the occupants to see out through uncurtained art glass windows and are situated high enough so outsiders cannot see inside the house.

LINCOLN PARK

This is Chicago's largest park and probably the most diversified in the amusements it provides. Miles of beaches. Two large yacht harbors. A world class zoo. Playing fields and facilties for baseball, cycling, softball, soccer, tennis, golf, volleyball, and rowing. And a wonderful collection of public sculpture, including **"The Standing Lincoln,"** by Augustus Saint-Gaudens, erected in 1887, and considered by many sculptors to be the best likeness of our sixteenth president and one of the finest works of monument art in the country. It may be found standing in front of the **Chicago History Museum** building at North Avenue and Clark Street. Also, see the **Ulysses S. Grant Memorial,** a large equestrian statue visible from Lake Shore Drive; and **William Shakespeare,** set in a small quiet garden across from the **Lincoln Park Conservatory**.

Left: The Lincoln Park lake shore with Diversey and Belmont Harbors.
Below: Lincoln Park Zoo—open 7 days a week and free for all.

Above: A green Chicago River is a St. Patrick's Day tradition.

Above left: Taste of Chicago in Grant Park delights and over-feeds thousands of hungry locals and visitors.

Below left: The Printers Row Book Fair attracts bargain hunters to the south Loop.

SPECIAL EVENTS AND FAIRS

Nothing in Chicago quite equals of **"Taste of Chicago,"** with its teeming masses of hungry families and cool teenagers "hanging out." **Taste** ends with a spectacular patriotic concert by the **Grant Park Symphony Orchestra** on the evening of July 3. The *1812 Overture* is traditionally played with spectacular fireworks exploding over the lake. But many other events are celebrated as well. All the big ethnic "days" have their parades, some in the Loop, some in neighborhoods. The most spectacular downtown parade is the **St. Patrick's Day Parade**, down Dearborn Street in the Loop in March. Bands, politicians—especially those *currently running for office*, floats, bagpipes, and, yes, the city does dye the river green—very green. Politically, Chicago is still an Irish town.

THE RESTAURANT SCENE

River North has become the restaurant district, offering everything from the **Hard Rock Cafe** to world famous deep dish Chicago style pizza from **Pizzeria Uno and Due**. For serious ethnic food, one needs to find Chinatown and Greektown. Some good Polish cooking is still served up on Milwaukee Avenue. Italian and Thai restaurants are everywhere in Chicago, as are Chinese and Mexican.

Top: Sidewalk cafes proliferate in summer. Middle (3): River North offers great variety in dining. Bottom left: Dining at the rivers edge is increasingly popular. Bottom right: Harry Carey's gone, but his restaurant lives on.

O'HARE INTERNATIONAL AIRPORT

After years of improvisation, Chicago's O'Hare Airport, located on the northwest corner of the city, can now truly be called **O'Hare International**. It competes with Atlanta's airport for the title of "busiest in the world." Yet, for all its largeness, there is demand for yet another airport in Chicago to supplement O'Hare and Midway (a smaller airport on the southwest side of the city). The Illinois General Assembly debates the issue annualy.

In the mid '90s, one of the most ambitious improvement programs ever undertaken by a major airport was completed. There is now a state-of-the-art International Terminal, totally separate from the domestic operation, and an inter-airport Electric Rail Transit System to connect the two. The terminal is vast, spread wide to accomodate the largest jets. Electric carts shuttle passengers to and from departure and arrival gates.

There are 156 ticketing positions on the departure level. Multiple Immigration and Customs stations greet arrivals and speed them through. As air traffic increases in the twenty-first century, O'Hare can still expand to handle additional traffic. Another runway is proposed.

A City Visitor Information Center is staffed with multi-lingual representatives. Fast, inexpensive CTA rail service connects O'Hare to the Loop.

Left: The Grand Concourse in the International Terminal.

Right and below: The north facade and the walkway from parking to the International Terminal.

INDEX